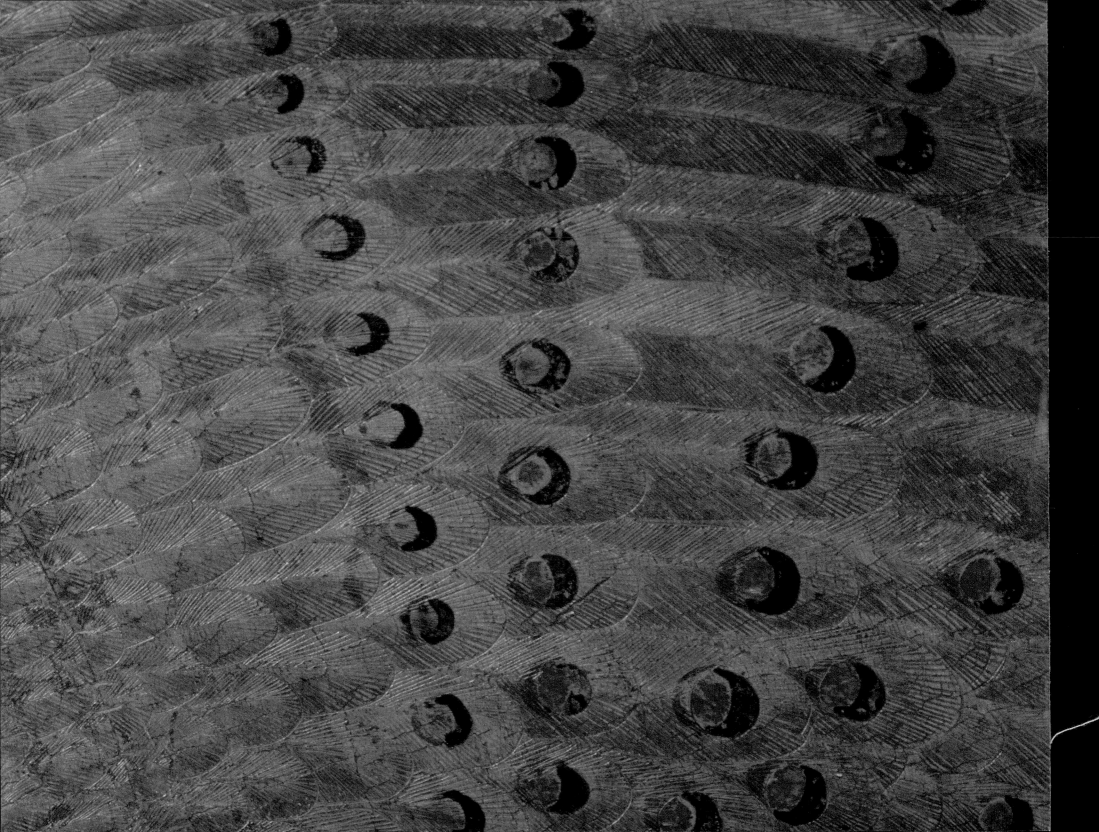

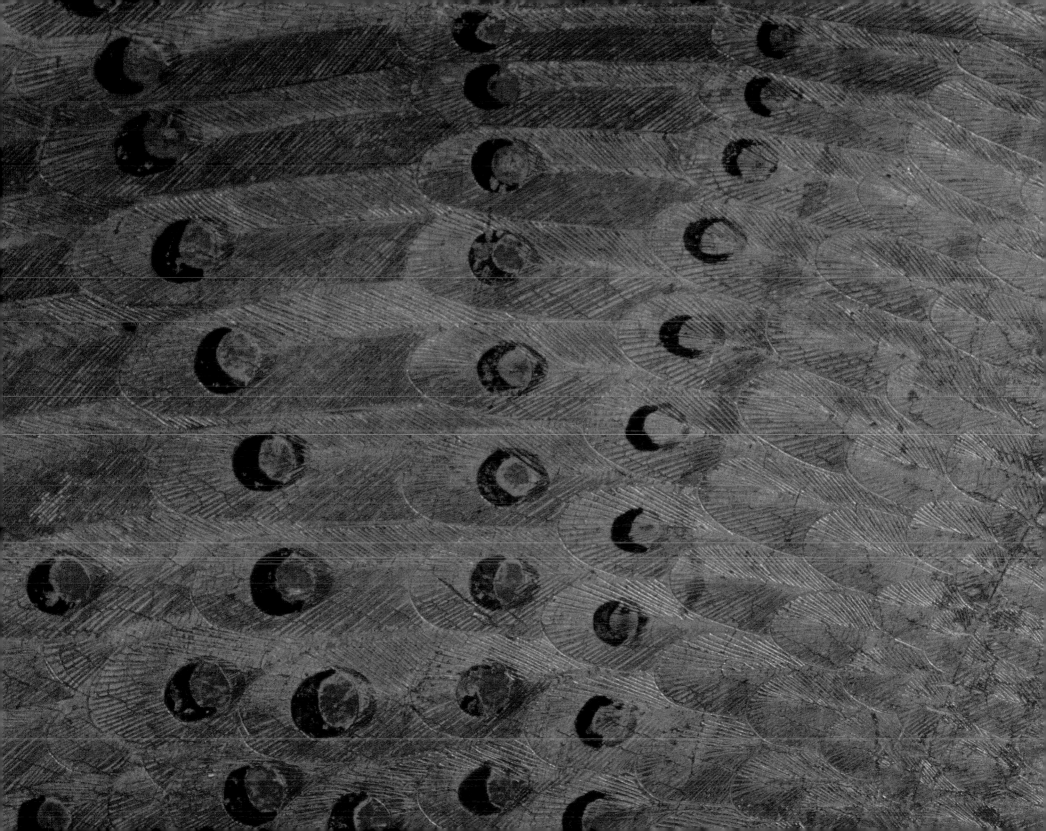

For unto us a child is born, unto us a son is given:
and the government shall be upon his shoulder: and his name
shall be called Wonderful, Counsellor, The mighty God,
The everlasting Father, The Prince of Peace.

THE FIRST CHRISTMAS

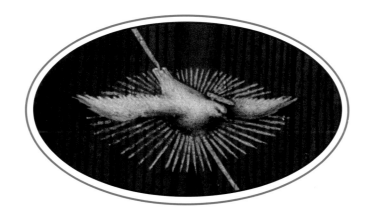

The words are taken from the Authorized King James Version of the Bible
from the Book of the Prophet Isaiah and the Gospels of St Matthew and St Luke.

THE FIRST CHRISTMAS

THE NATIONAL GALLERY, LONDON

Frances Lincoln

in association with

National Gallery Publications, London

And in the sixth month the angel Gabriel was sent from God unto a city of Galilee, named Nazareth, to a virgin espoused to a man whose name was Joseph, of the house of David; and the virgin's name was Mary.

And the angel came in unto her, and said,

"Hail, thou that art highly favoured, the Lord is with thee: blessed art thou among women."

And when she saw him, she was troubled at his saying, and cast in her mind what manner of salutation this should be.

And the angel said unto her,

"Fear not, Mary: for thou hast found favour with God. And, behold, thou shalt conceive in thy womb, and bring forth a son, and shalt call his name JESUS. He shall be great, and shall be called the Son of the Highest: and the Lord God shall give unto him the throne of his father David: and he shall reign over the house of Jacob for ever; and of his kingdom there shall be no end."

And Mary said,

"Behold the handmaid of the Lord; be it unto me according to thy word."

And the angel departed from her.

And it came to pass in those days that there went out a decree from Caesar Augustus, that all the world should be taxed.

And all went to be taxed, every one into his own city. And Joseph also went up from Galilee, out of the city of Nazareth, into Judaea, unto the city of David, which is called Bethlehem (because he was of the house and lineage of David): to be taxed with Mary his espoused wife, being great with child.

And so it was, that, while they were there, the days were accomplished that she should be delivered. And she brought forth her firstborn son, and wrapped him in swaddling clothes, and laid him in a manger; because there was no room for them in the inn.

And there were in the same country shepherds abiding in the field, keeping watch over their flock by night. And, lo, the angel of the Lord came upon them, and the glory of the Lord shone round about them: and they were sore afraid. And the angel said unto them,

"Fear not: for, behold, I bring you good tidings of great joy, which shall be to all people. For unto you is born this day in the city of David a Saviour, which is Christ the Lord. And this shall be a sign unto you; ye shall find the babe wrapped in swaddling clothes, lying in a manger."

And suddenly there was with the angel a multitude of the heavenly host praising God, and saying,

"Glory to God in the highest, and on earth peace, good will toward men."

And it came to pass, as the angels were gone away from them into heaven, the shepherds said one to another,

"Let us now go even unto Bethlehem, and see this thing which is come to pass, which the Lord hath made known unto us."

And they came with haste, and found Mary, and Joseph, and the babe lying in a manger. And when they had seen it, they made known abroad the saying which was told them concerning this child.

Now when Jesus was born in Bethlehem of Judaea in the days of Herod the king, behold, there came wise men from the east to Jerusalem, saying,

"Where is he that is born King of the Jews? for we have seen his star in the east, and are come to worship him."

Then Herod, when he had privily called the wise men, enquired of them diligently what time the star appeared. And he sent them to Bethlehem, and said, "Go and search diligently for the young child; and when ye have found him, bring me word again, that I may come and worship him also."

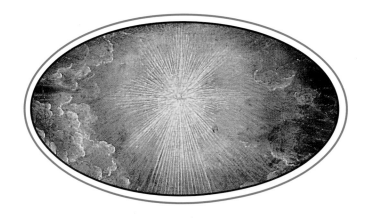

When they had heard the king, they departed; and, lo, the star, which they saw in the east, went before them, till it came and stood over where the young child was.

When they saw the star, they rejoiced with exceeding great joy. And when they were come into the house, they saw the young child with Mary his mother, and fell down, and worshipped him: and when they had opened their treasures, they presented unto him gifts; gold, and frankincense, and myrrh. And being warned of God in a dream that they should not return to Herod, they departed into their own country another way.

And when they were departed, behold, the angel of the Lord appeareth to Joseph in a dream, saying, "Arise, and take the young child and his mother, and flee into Egypt, and be thou there until I bring thee word: for Herod will seek the young child to destroy him."

When he arose, he took the young child and his mother by night, and departed into Egypt.

Index

The illustrations are details of the following paintings.

The Adoration of the Kings
Follower of Fra Angelico
(around 1450)
The King kneeling to kiss the
Child's foot has handed his gift
to Joseph.

Back cover
A Choir of Angels
Simon Marmion
(active 1449; died 1489)
Marmion worked in France and
Flanders. He painted altarpieces –
panels for altars – and was also a
miniaturist and a painter of
manuscripts, which explains the fine
detail and delicacy of his work.

Endpapers
Altarpiece: The Annunciation
Follower of Fra Angelico
(around 1450)
As one of the most significant
episodes from the Virgin's life the
Annunciation was often the main
subject of an altarpiece. Notice
the delicate colour and the
brilliant light.

Page 5 (half-title)
*The Virgin and Child
with Four Saints*
Francesco Bonsignori
(?1455-1519)
Bonsignori worked in Verona and
Mantua. This painting is based on
an engraving (made by cutting a
design on a hard surface which is
then printed) by the Italian artist
Mantegna (1430/31-1506).

Page 6 (opposite title page)
The Annunciation, with St Emidius
Carlo Crivelli
(active 1457-93)
Crivelli was a Venetian painter living
in Ascoli. The picture shows the
patron saint of Ascoli, Saint
Emidius, who carries a model of the
town, waylaying the angel Gabriel as
he goes to the Virgin.

Page 7 (title page)
The Annunciation
Fra Filippo Lippi
(about 1406-69)
Lippi, a Carmelite friar from
Florence, almost certainly painted
this panel for the Medici, Florence's
ruling family. Its shape suggests that
it may have been painted for a
bedroom.

Page 11
The Annunciation
Lippi
See the entry for page 7.

Page 13
*The Virgin and Child
in a Landscape*
Netherlandish School
(early 16th century)
Round pictures were painted less
often by painters in the Netherlands
than by the Italians. The town in the
background is probably Bruges.

Page 8
The Annunciation, with St Emidius
Crivelli
See the entry for page 6.

Page 9
Altarpiece: The Annunciation
Follower of Fra Angelico
See the entry for the endpapers.

Page 14
"Mystic Nativity"
Sandro Botticelli
(?1445-1510)
In Botticelli's unconventional
treatment of the subject, the Virgin
is larger than the other figures.
Angels broadcast news of Christ's
coming and the prospect of Peace
on Earth; the devils scatter.

Page 12
The Adoration of the Kings
Giorgione
(active 1506; died 1510)
The artist, born in Castelfranco
and nicknamed "Big George",
was famous in his own time,
but little is now known
about his life. He produced
dreamy paintings with soft
colour and light.

Page 15

The Nativity, at Night

Ascribed to Geertgen tot Sint Jans
(?1455/65-85/95)

Geertgen's use of dramatic light was exceptional for his time. Here, the night is lit both by the Infant and by the angel in the background who casts light over the shepherd and flock.

Pages 18 and 19

The Adoration of the Shepherds

Guido Reni
(1575-1642)

The painter was born in Bologna and worked all over Italy. His art is full of grace and sweetness. Other artists may have worked on parts of this large picture – it is 3 metres wide and over 4 metres high.

Page 17

The Adoration of the Kings

Jan Gossaert
(active 1503; died 1532)

Jan Gossaert was a Netherlandish painter whose work shows a strong interest in Italian painting. Notice how the back of the work gets lighter as the angels get smaller, creating an impression of distance.

Page 20

The Adoration of the Kings

Gossaert

See the entry for page 17.

Page 21

Altarpiece: The Adoration of the Kings

Vincenzo Foppa
(active 1456; died 1515/16)

He was the leading painter in North Italy. Foppa became interested in *atmospheric* perspective – showing far distances by using paler tones towards the horizon.

Page 22

The Adoration of the Kings
Gerard David
(active from 1484; died 1523)
The most important artist working
in Bruges in the early sixteenth
century. His work is full of rich
colours and precise detail.

Page 23

The Adoration of the Kings
Foppa
See the entry for page 21.

Page 24

The Flight into Egypt
Master of 1518
This is a panel from a wooden
altarpiece painted by an artist from
Antwerp. Some altarpieces have
painted movable panels that close
over the main picture.

Page 25

*The Rest on the Flight
into Egypt*
Pierre Patel
(about 1606-76)
Patel was probably born in northern
France. He was influenced by the
classical landscapes of the French
painter Claude Lorrain – the Holy
Family rests against derelict ruins
while behind them the view opens
between the trees to the sea.

Extracts from the Authorized Version of the Bible
(the King James Bible), the rights in which are vested
in the Crown, are reproduced by permission of the
Crown's patentee, Cambridge University Press.

Text and illustrations copyright © Frances Lincoln Limited 1992
Illustrations copyright © National Gallery 1992

First published in Great Britain in 1992 by
Frances Lincoln Children's Books, 4 Torriano Mews,
Torriano Avenue, London NW5 2RZ
www.franceslincoln.com

This edition published in Great Britain in 2009
and in the USA in 2010

British Library Cataloguing in Publication Data
available on request

ISBN 978-1-84780-001-5

Set in Cloister Roman

Printed in China

9 8 7 6 5 4 3 2 1

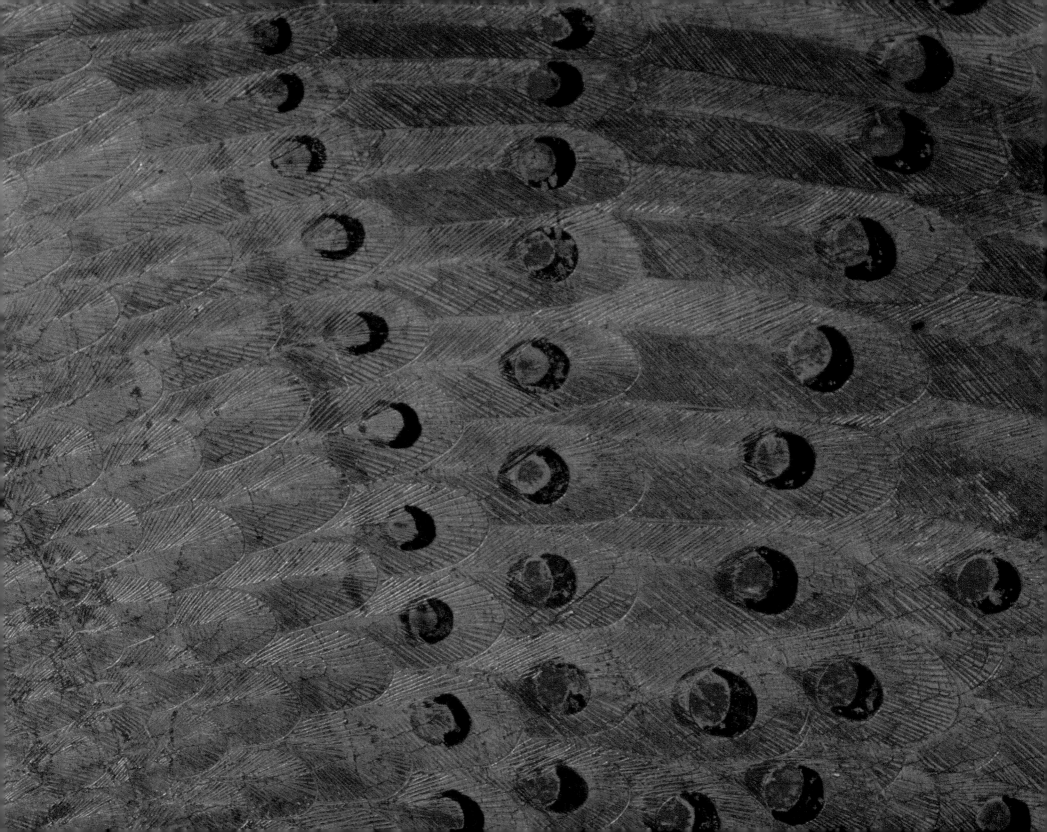

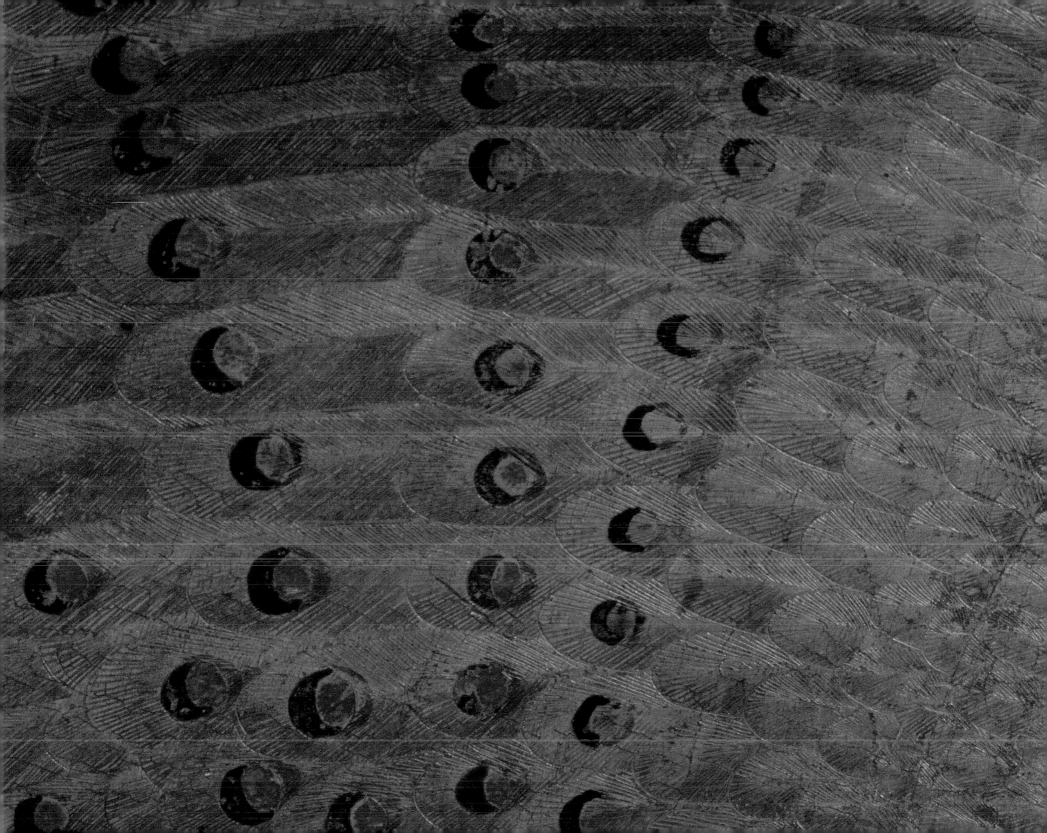

MORE TITLES FROM FRANCES LINCOLN CHILDREN'S BOOKS

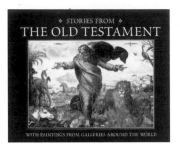

Stories from the Old Testament
With paintings from galleries around the world

This collection brings together 17 of the best-known stories from the Old Testament, told in the resonant language of the King James Bible, and illustrated with masterpieces from a selection of the world's greatest painters.

The Nativity
Francesca Crespi

Six 3-D tableaux portray the story of the birth of Jesus in this simple and elegant retelling. Each scene has tabs to pull, moving parts, screens that unfold, and, in a splendid finale, double doors that open wide to reveal the full glory of the Nativity.

Ding Dong! Merrily on High
Francesca Crespi

Here, beautifully presented in 3-D pop-ups, are five familiar and much-loved carols: O Christmas Tree, Silent Night, We Three Kings, Hark the Herald Angels Sing and Ding Dong Merrily on High. Complemented by the melody line and guitar chords, these carols evoke the traditional spirit of Christmas.

Frances Lincoln titles are available from all good bookshops.
You can also buy books and find out more about your favourite titles,
authors and illustrators on our website: www.franceslincoln.com